MARKS

of a

DISCIPLE

Six Measurements for Growth

Dean Inserra

Lifeway Press®
Nashville, Tennessee

Editorial Team

Reid Patton
Writer

Susan Hill
Production Editor

Jon Rodda
Art Director

Joel Polk
Editorial Team Leader

Brian Daniel
Manager, Adult Discipleship

Brandon Hiltibidal
Director, Adult Ministry

Published by Lifeway Press® • © 2021 Dean Inserra

No part of this book may be reproduced or transmitted in any form or by any means, electronic or mechanical, including photocopying and recording, or by any information storage or retrieval system, except as may be expressly permitted in writing by the publisher. Requests for permission should be addressed in writing to Lifeway Press®; One Lifeway Plaza; Nashville, TN 37234.

ISBN 978-1-5359-7866-8 • Item Number 005819225

DEWEY: 248.84

SUBHD: DISCIPLESHIP / CHRISTIAN LIFE / SPIRITUAL LIFE

Unless otherwise noted, all Scripture quotations are taken from the Christian Standard Bible®, Copyright © 2017 by Holman Bible Publishers. Used by permission. Christian Standard Bible® and CSB® are federally registered trademarks of Holman Bible Publishers.

Scripture quotations marked (NIV) are taken from the Holy Bible, New International Version®, NIV®. Copyright © 1973, 1978, 1984, 2011 by Biblica, Inc.TM Used by permission of Zondervan. All rights reserved worldwide. www.zondervan.com. The "NIV" and "New International Version" are trademarks registered in the United States Patent and Trademark Office by Biblica, Inc.TM

To order additional copies of this resource, write to Lifeway Resources Customer Service; One Lifeway Plaza; Nashville, TN 37234; fax 615-251-5933; call toll free 800-458-2772; order online at Lifeway.com; or email orderentry@lifeway.com.

Printed in the United States of America

Adult Ministry Publishing • Lifeway Resources • One Lifeway Plaza • Nashville, TN 37234

CONTENTS

Marks of a Disciple

ABOUT THE AUTHOR

Dean Inserra is the founding and lead pastor of CITYCHURCH, where he leads the vision and preaching. Dean was called to start a church in his hometown of Tallahassee when he was the Student Body President at Leon High School. He is passionate about reaching the city of Tallahassee with the gospel, to see a worldwide impact made for Jesus.

Dean graduated from Liberty University and attended Southern Baptist Theological Seminary in Louisville, KY. He holds a MA in Theological Studies from Midwestern Baptist Theological Seminary and is pursuing a D. Min from Southern Seminary.

Dean is an advisory member of the Ethics and Religious Liberty Commission's Leadership Council with the Southern Baptist Convention. He is also a member of Baptist 21.

Dean is married to Krissie, and they have two sons, Tommy and Ty, and a daughter, Sally Ashlyn. Dean likes baseball, wrestling, and the Miami Hurricanes. He believes Tom Brady is the greatest quarterback, and that everyone who disagrees holds the right to be wrong.

HOW TO GET THE MOST FROM THIS STUDY

This Bible study book includes six weeks of content for group and personal study.

Group Sessions

Regardless of what day of the week your group meets, each week of content begins with the group session. Each group session uses the following format to facilitate simple yet meaningful interaction among group members, with God's Word, and with the teaching from Dean Inserra.

START. This page includes questions to get the conversation started and to introduce the video teaching.

WATCH. This page is intentionally left blank to take notes during the video teaching.

DISCUSS. This page includes questions and statements that guide the group to respond to Dean's video teaching and to explore relevant Bible passages.

DURING THE NEXT WEEK. This section gives group members something to think about over the next week. This includes directions, a few questions, and a verse of Scripture to memorize.

Personal Study

Personal Evaluation

Each session gives group members the opportunity to examine their lives and see how committed they are to the mark of a disciple being discussed in that session. Don't let this section make you feel guilty or that you have to do more, rather, let it guide you to healthier spiritual practices.

Bible Study

Each week provides two days of Bible study and learning activities for individual engagement between group sessions. The personal study revisits stories, Scriptures, and themes Dean introduced in the videos so that participants can understand and apply them on a personal level. Each day of personal study ends with a key question.

Marks of a Disciple

Session 1
REPENTANT LIFE

Start
Welcome to Session 1

When you have a child, each year of their lives they have a physical and a doctor examines them to ensure they're hitting certain milestones. This kind of evaluation is normal and healthy. *Marks of a Disciple* is all about identifying six marks or measurements of our faith so we can know if we're progressing in our faith. We're going to start this session with the first mark: a repentant life.

When do you first remember hearing the word "repentance?"

What do we typically associate with this word?

Most of the time when we hear the word *repentance*, we are conditioned to think about the initial moment of repentance when we begin following Jesus. Growing Christians live a life of repentance. It's not a milestone you reach or a destination that you accomplish and check off your list. Growing Christians are repentant Christians.

Ask someone to pray, then watch the session 1 video together.

Watch

Use this space to take notes during the video teaching.

Discuss
Read Romans 2:4 together.

> Or do you despise the riches of his kindness, restraint, and patience, not
> recognizing that God's kindness is intended to lead you to repentance?
> **ROMANS 2:4**

Dean defined repentance as, "a response to the goodness, kindness, and grace of God in
our lives." However, there are two lies that keep us from embracing a life of repentance.
The first is the false belief that we gain more by disobeying God than by obeying Him. The
second lie tells us that we have to go around God for the things we want in life. Both of
these lies keep us from experiencing the grace of God found in repentance.

1. How did the video teaching challenge your thinking about
   repentance?

2. Why do we tend to think of repentance as a one time action, rather
   than an ongoing posture toward God?

3. How is repentance related to God's kindness? How does repentance
   lead us into a deeper relationship with God?

4. Why do many of us struggle with the two lies Dean discussed?

5. Read Genesis 3:1-7. Why did Adam and Eve feel the need to go
   around God to get what they wanted? When are you most tempted
   to do the same?

6. What are some areas of our lives where we delay repentance? Why?

Close your time together in prayer

During the Next Week

1. Complete the two personal studies and evaluation.

2. Pray and ask God to reveal areas where you need to repent and return to Him.

3. Begin each day committed to live with a posture of repentance.

4. As you go through the day, embrace opportunities to repent.

5. Memorize Romans 2:4.

Evaluation

Use the following questions to help you recognize
this mark of a disciple in your life.

Do you desire to experience God's kindness through repentance? If yes, how
did you come to desire this? If not, what is holding you back?

What areas of your life are you most tempted to work around God
to get what you want?

What areas are you most tempted to reduce repentance to a checklist?

How often is your prayer life characterized by repentance? Do you need to make any changes? Explain.

What do you need to repent of right now?

Personal Study 1

INITIAL REPENTANCE

Today, we're going to define repentance and examine why it is essential in the life of a Christian. Repentance is the entry point into the Christian life. The entirety of the Christian life flows from one initial act of repentance.

What thoughts or images come to your mind when you hear the word "repent"?

How would you define repentance?

Repentance is one of those words we use without giving much thought to what it means. The historic confession of faith, the Westminster Shorter Catechism answers the question "What is repentance?" this way:

> Repentance unto life is a saving grace, whereby a sinner out of a true sense of his sin and apprehension of the mercy of God in Christ, doth with grief and hatred of his sin, turn from it unto God, with full purpose of an endeavor after new obedience.

If that language is a little lofty to you, let's break it down further. Repentance is turning *from* your sins *to* God. Paul wrote that repentance is actually a response to God's kindness.

> Or do you despise the riches of his kindness, restraint, and patience, not recognizing that God's kindness is intended to lead you to repentance?
> **ROMANS 2:4**

Look at your earlier definition of repentance. How might you adjust your definition based on what you just read?

Repentance is not God calling you to a list of rules; He's calling you to Himself. He's inviting you to His kindness, patience, and restraint. He's inviting you to enter into a relationship with Him. When we think about repentance this way it becomes an invitation to experience God's character.

Responding to God's Invitation

Read Romans 2:5-8.

To know God is to know God's mercy. Even people who don't follow God want God to be loving and kind. But if you deny your need to repent you are "despising" the mercy of God. Once you truly understand the depth of your need, you will run to God's mercy. Repentance unleashes God's kindness in our lives.

Based upon these verses, why is repentance necessary?

What awaits us if we continue to live without seeking repentance?

Our sin deserves judgment and we desperately need God's mercy. The mercy we need can only be found in Jesus. He is the only One who never needed to repent because He perfectly kept God's law. In His kindness, God shelters us from the judgment we deserved by placing it on Jesus. He offers us forgiveness if we turn from our sins and place our trust in Him.

Have you ever come to a moment when you repented of your sins and turned to Jesus? If not, what is stopping you from doing so right now?

Experiencing God's Kindness

How does repentance allow us to experience God's kindness, restraint, and patience?

God will judge sin, but He also shows us kindness, restraint, and patience. He demonstrates His kindness by encouraging us to come to Him, He shows restraint when He doesn't treat us as our sins deserve, and He shows patience as we experience failures. God walks with us, loves us, and He calls us His sons and His daughters. Now God's grace toward us is a defining feature of our lives.

Read Ephesians 2:4-9.

If you know Jesus, make a list of what is true about you by making "I am" statements in the space below. List at least three.

I am...

I am...

I am...

For the disciple, repentance and faith in Jesus are inextricably connected. To repent of your sins is to trust in Jesus. They are unified actions. The Books of Ephesians tells us repentance is given to us so that God "might display the immeasurable riches of his grace through his kindness to us in Christ Jesus" (v. 7). Paul used the same word for kindness in Ephesians 2:7 and Romans 2:4. God's kindness should change us and lead us into a growing relationship with Jesus.

In Closing

What does a lifestyle of repentance look like in the life of a believer?

How is God's kindness motivating you to extend grace and mercy toward others?

Personal Study 2

ONGOING REPENTANCE

On October 31, 1517 a German monk by the name of Martin Luther nailed his *Ninety-Five Theses* on the door of the All Saints' Church in Wittenberg, Germany, igniting the Protestant Reformation. While you may have learned about this event in your middle school history class, you might be less familiar with what Luther's document says. Luther's first thesis reads:

> When our Lord and master Jesus Christ said, "Repent (Matt. 4:17)." He willed the entire life of believers to be one of repentance.

Luther and the other Protestant reformers argued repentance is not just the entry point into the Christian life, but the whole of Christian life. Following Jesus means our lives are being consistently transformed by His grace. Therefore, we repent often.

What happens to our faith if we begin to treat repentance as optional?

Do you know anyone who models a life of repentance? What is different about their life? What could you learn from them?

Repentance is not a box to check, nor is it God's way of spanking us with a wooden spoon when we're bad. Rather, it's God's loving pursuit of you—an invitation to change that we must accept over and over again. To decline God's invitation is to despise and reject the grace of God. The Bible helps us see what ongoing repentance looks like in practice.

Guided by the Scripture

David wrote:

> Search me, God, and know my heart;
> test me and know my concerns.
> See if there is any offensive way in me;
> lead me in the everlasting way.
> **PSALM 139:23-24**

List the requests given in this psalm.

Why are prayers like these a mark of Christian maturity?

David invited God to search his heart, diagnose his motives, and lead him back into a life pleasing to God. David understood he needed God's help to see himself clearly. Christian maturity is not merely the ability to resist sin, but also what we do in response to our sins. While we should certainly try and resist sin, there will be times we ultimately fail. In those moments, we can choose to go on with our lives or to approach God with repentance and receive His forgiveness.

If going to God with your sin is a mark of maturity, how might an immature Christian handle their sin?

Transformed Instead of Conformed

When we embrace repentance as a daily reality, it changes the way we live because it changes the way we worship as we are conformed into the image of Christ. Consider Paul's words:

> Therefore, brothers and sisters, in view of the mercies of God, I urge you to present your bodies as a living sacrifice, holy and pleasing to God; this is your true worship. Do not be conformed to this age, but be transformed by the renewing of your mind, so that you may discern what is the good, pleasing, and perfect will of God.
> **ROMANS 12:1-2**

What are some ways we are "conformed to this age"? Give practical examples.

What does our culture tell you to do with your sin? How does the message our culture preaches contrast with what you've learned this week?

While the world tells us to "follow our hearts," Scripture tells us our hearts are deceitful above all else (Jer. 17:9). "Embrace your truth" has become a cultural mantra, but the Bible tells us that truth is found not in us, but in the person and work of Jesus. Being conformed to the world means embracing our sin and excusing its entanglements. Paul points us to a better way.

How have your desires changed as you have followed God?

How have those changes produced growth and maturity in you?

Repentance means instead of being conformed to the world and its desires, we are transformed as our minds are renewed. A shift begins to take place in our loyalties. We exchange the desires of this world for new loyalties toward God.

In Closing

Spend a few moments asking God to examine your heart
and motives. Write down what He reveals to you.

Spend a few more moments receiving God's
cleansing and His forgiveness.

Marks of a Disciple

Session 2
HEALTHY HABITS

Start
Welcome to Session 2.

Last session we talked about how living a repentant life is an important marker of our spiritual health. Let's begin by reflecting back on what we learned.

How did our last session lead you to think differently about repentance?

If repentance is the foundation for the Christian life, healthy habits provide the support and structure for a Christian life. We learn the importance of habits early on. Anyone who has parented an infant knows how important structure is to his or her young life. Helping babies learn the rhythms of eating and sleeping is crucial to the baby's health and the parents' sanity.

What is a personal habit that has helped you in life?

What is a spiritual habit you would like to develop?

While we're no longer dependent upon others to set our habits for us, our habits continue to shape and inform the way we spend our time and the choices we make. This session is all about how healthy spiritual habits are a marker for spiritual health.

Ask someone to pray then watch the session 2 video together.

Watch

Use this space to take notes during the video teaching.

Discuss
Read 2 Peter 3:18 together.

> But grow in the grace and knowledge of our Lord and Savior Jesus
> Christ. To him be the glory both now and to the day of eternity.
> **2 PETER 3:18**

Dean taught God has given us three channels of grace—His voice (Scriptures), His ear (prayer), and His body (the local church)—to grow as a Christian. We utilize these channels by pursuing healthy spiritual habits.

1. Read 1 Peter 2:2 (NIV). What does it look like to "crave" the Scriptures? How do we get to that place as believers?

2. How does prayer increase our dependence upon and trust in God? Share examples from your prayer life.

3. How often do you pray during a 24-hour period? What might it look like for you to begin to pray without ceasing (1 Thess. 5:17)?

4. How does our involvement in the local church increase our awareness of God's voice and God's ear?

5. What are some common excuses we give for not utilizing the channels of grace God has given us? How can we overcome these excuses?

6. Your habits may help or encourage someone else. Share some ways you have benefited from Scripture reading, prayer, and involvement in your local church.

Close your time together in prayer

During the Next Week

1. Complete the two personal studies and evaluation on the following pages.

2. Spend 10 minutes each day reading your Bible.

3. Schedule several times to pause and pray this week.

4. If you do not have a local church, decide to be committed to one.

5. Memorize 2 Peter 3:18.

Evaluation

Use the following questions to help you recognize
this mark of a disciple in your life.

Of the spiritual disciplines we're studying this week—Scripture reading, prayer,
and involvement in a local church—which one do you engage most regularly?
Which one(s) would you like to see growth?

Spend a few moments evaluating your weekly and monthly schedule. Where
can you make time and space to engage the Lord through healthy habits?
What might you need to cut to make time and space?

How meaningful is your time in God's Word? What changes do you need to
make to this time? If this is not a regular habit of yours, how might you start?

Think about the rhythms of prayer in your life. Is prayer a regular part of your day or is it an addendum that's engaged when needed? What changes do you need to make?

How are you involved and serving at your local church? Where are you using the gifts and talents the Lord has given you?

Personal Study 1

HABITS THAT FORM US
PART 1

The central premise Jame Clear's best-selling book, *Atomic Habits,* is that the habits we embrace form the kind of person we become. According to Clear: "Habits are the small decisions you make and actions you perform every day.[1]" While we are more than the sum of our habits, Clear has a point. A person who exercises regularly is generally healthier than someone who doesn't. Students who devote time to study tend to have better GPAs than their peers. Christians of every age and every demographic are designed by God to grow in their faith. Healthy habits, or spiritual disciplines, are the practices God has given us to grow our faith. However, before we look at individual habits, it may be helpful to consider why we need habits at all.

Why Habits?

Read 2 Peter 3:18.

What does it mean to "grow in the grace" of Jesus? How do we do this?

How is growing in grace different than building a competency or skill?

The last words in Peter's second letter to the church were a command to grow in the grace and knowledge of Jesus. We can learn several important truths from this short verse. First, notice what we're called to—grace. Grace by definition is unmerited favor, it's something we receive from God and is independent from anything we have in ourselves. Earlier in 2 Peter, he wrote that God "has given us everything required for life and godliness" (1:3). Unlike other habits, our growth in grace doesn't happen by our own effort, but by God's power.

How does the process of developing healthy spiritual habits change when you realize they are given by God's grace?

Second, Christian growth is continual. In the original language of the New Testament, the word "grow" is an active imperative. In other words, it's an action that's meant to be ongoing in the life of a Christian. Unlike a fad diet meant to produce specific results over a period of time, spiritual disciplines are habits for life given to us to help us know God.

According to Peter, what is the goal of healthy habits? Why does that matter?

Lastly, the object of spiritual habits is God. Peter ends the verse we're examining—and a letter about Christian growth—with praise to God. We cultivate healthy habits, because God is worthy to be known. The growth process is governed by grace, but requires our effort. Hosea said, "Let's strive to know the LORD" (6:3). Paul urged us to "train" ourselves "in godliness" (1 Tim. 4:7). Remember the goal is to grow in your faith, not to feel less guilty. Our habits have an object—Jesus. All spiritual habits help us know and enjoy Jesus more.

God's Voice

Read 2 Timothy 3:16-17.

Why do we need the Bible to hear God's voice?

All effort to grow in grace begins with hearing God's voice through the Scriptures. We hear God's voice when we read the Bible. We don't need to go look for extra words from God. That doesn't mean He doesn't speak other ways; however, the only way we can know for sure that God is speaking is by reading His Word. Only the Bible is "inspired" by God.

Why is the Bible necessary for our growth in the grace and knowledge of Jesus Christ?

The Bible is profitable for us because it faithfully communicates God's character. To grow in the grace and knowledge of Jesus Christ, we have to know Jesus Christ. He has revealed Himself so that we can know Him, understand who He is, and how we've rebelled against Him. The Bible communicates God's plan to reconcile people to Himself. He's expressed that to us in human words because He wants us to know Him. Let's consider a few different strategies to regularly hear from God through His Word.

Engaging God's Voice

MAKE A PLAN. If you've never established a Bible reading habit, it's helpful to formulate a plan. Start by finding a time and a place where you can be alone and undistracted. For some people that's first thing in the morning, for others, it's later in the day, or maybe it's a different time each day. Lastly, choose a place to start in Scripture. If you're unfamiliar with the Bible, start with one of the Gospels—Matthew, Mark, Luke, or John. Read one chapter a day and spend time reflecting on what you've read.

When and where will you read Scripture? Set a place and a time.

What will you read in Scripture. Choose a book of the Bible.

STUDY. In addition to reading God's Word, we should make time to study it. Study happens when we carefully read and reread the passage and we make observations. We might ask questions like, "Who is speaking?" "Who is being addressed?" "What did the original author indent to communicate to his readers?" These are not the only questions worth asking, but they are a good starting place.

> **Take a few minutes and read and reread 2 Timothy 3:16-17. Write down one detail that became clearer to you after multiple readings.**

APPLY THE WORD. God has spoken to us through the Bible, so reading the Bible should change our lives. Any time we read Scripture we should always consider how God might want us to change or what He might want us to do as a result of what we have read.

> **Reread 2 Peter 3:18 and 2 Timothy 3:16-17.**
> **How should you apply the truths of these verses today?**

In Closing

Who might encourage you and motivate you as you read? Identify one friend and share what you're doing. Ask them to hold you accountable.

---

[1] James Clear, "Habits Guide: How to Build Good Habits and Break Bad Ones," November 11, 2020, jamesclear.com/habits.

Personal Study 2

HABITS THAT FORM US
PART 2

In the last personal study, we considered how habits help us grow in the grace of Jesus Christ, and we took a deeper look at Bible reading. In this study, we're going to examine two more habits–prayer and involvement in a local church. But before we do that. Let's take a moment to see where all of these habits fit into the life of the first church.

Read Acts 2:42.

What spiritual habits do you notice in the life of the early church?

How do these habits compare with the habits in your life or the life of your local church?

This verse follows Peter's sermon on Pentecost where Scripture tells us "about three thousand people" believed the gospel (Acts 2:41). The "they" in verse 42 are those believers who constituted the newly formed church. The first thing Luke tells us about the church is about the spiritual habits they devoted themselves to. Notice they took time to hear from the apostles' teaching (the Scriptures), to pray, and to fellowship (involvement in the local church). These have been the channels of grace God has used since the beginning. Let's look at the remaining disciplines individually.

God's Ear

What do you believe happens when we pray?

Our God who speaks to us in Scripture is also a God who listens in prayer. Simply defined, prayer is speaking to God. In prayer God allows us to share our cares, needs, and worship in accordance with His will. Furthermore, our prayers are the means by which God accomplishes His will on earth.

How should knowing God uses our prayers to enact His will change the way we pray?

Engaging God's Ear

SCHEDULE TIME. Many of us would admit we struggle with prayer. That's normal. Thankfully, routines and habits are our friends in the Christian life. If prayer is a struggle for you, schedule time to pray and don't feel bad about that. Nowhere in the Bible does it say if it's not spontaneous then it's not legit.

When and where could you schedule time for prayer?

UTILIZE PRAYERS FROM SCRIPTURE. God's Word is filled with prayers. Jesus actually said "you should pray like this" (Matt. 6:9-15). Paul frequently prayed for the church (see Phil. 1:9-11; Eph. 3:14-21). The psalms are filled with prayers. We can pray these inspired prayers.

Pick a favorite psalm or one of the prayers cited above and pray for a few minutes using them as a guide.

PRAY TO GOD ABOUT GOD. We typically think of prayers as being a list of requests or a confession of sin. Yet, most of the prayers in the Bible are about God. Take the time to worship God through prayer and confess His character and reflect on His goodness.

What about God inspires you to worship Him? Offer a prayer to God thanking Him for who He is.

God's Body

Look at Acts 2:42 again. Luke writes that the early believers were devoted to fellowship and breaking of bread. Continuing through the Book of Acts, this devotion is carried out as the apostles established churches. The entire New Testament was written to churches. You won't find many verses that say "go join a church" because every letter in the New Testament assumes that Christians are part of a local church.

Read Acts 20:28. What does this verse teach us about the church?

Why should the church be important to every believer?

Church is a gathering of God's people who are established together under elders with a common belief and a common mission. The church was purchased by Jesus with His blood. As Christians who are growing, we should love what Jesus loves. And He loves the church with all the church's faults and failures. To be hostile to the church is to disregard what Jesus loves.

What does it look like to make the church a habit in your spiritual life?

What would it look like to neglect the local church?

Engaging God's Body

COMMIT. Being a Christian means being part of a local church. Commitment to the local church means going beyond attending to being a member of one specific body of believers. Listening to a pastor you like on a podcast every week or watching a church service on YouTube is not the same as being part of a local church. In addition to being God's body, the church is also referred to as a family (Gal. 6:10; Eph. 2:19). To be family, we have to know and be known by others. To be known, you have to show up, week after week.

Are you a member of a local church? If not, why not? If so, how has church membership contributed to your spiritual health?

SERVE. The church is a body and every part of the body is important (1 Cor. 12:12). We all bring unique gifts and talents to the church. If we don't use them, our local church will miss the gifts we have given to contribute. These gifts are varied and each one is needed. Engaging God's body means we develop the habit of serving regularly in the church.

What gifts has God given you to serve the church? How can you use them at your local church?

In Closing

What prayers do you need to offer to God today?

What is one way you can encourage someone in your church family this week?

Marks of a Disciple

Session 3
ETERNALLY MINDED

Start
Welcome to Session 3.

Last session we talked about cultivating healthy spiritual habits. However, talking about healthy habits isn't enough, we must incorporate them into the rhythms of our lives. Let's briefly consider last session's personal studies.

> **Look back through the previous two personal studies. Which tip for developing healthy habits did you find most useful?**

Spiritual habits increase our dependency on God and give us a greater vision for who He is. As our view of God grows, we will begin to naturally desire what He wants and live in accordance with His will (Ps. 37:4). This is the essence of what it means to be eternally minded—our next mark of a disciple.

> **How has your affection for God grown as you've followed Him?**

Disciples who are eternally minded think less of themselves and more of God. As we grow to be more eternally minded, we hold loosely to the things of this world and cling tightly to our citizenship in heaven.

Ask someone to pray, then watch the session 3 video together.

Watch

Use this space to take notes during the video teaching.

Discuss
Read Philippians 3:18-20.

> For I have often told you, and now say again with tears, that many
> live as enemies of the cross of Christ. Their end is destruction;
> their god is their stomach; their glory is in their shame; and they
> are focused on earthly things. Our citizenship is in heaven, and
> we eagerly wait for a Savior from there, the Lord Jesus Christ.
> **PHILIPPIANS 3:18-20**

Being eternally minded means that our primary concern is Christ and His coming kingdom. While we shouldn't remove ourselves from the world, we don't want to resemble the world either. Rather, we remember our citizenship in heaven and see all of life on earth through that lens.

1. What does the Bible mean when it calls us citizens of heaven and sojourners and exiles on earth (1 Pet. 2:11, NIV)?

2. How do the cultural messages of happiness and self-fulfillment cause us to lose sight of our citizenship in heaven? Where has this mindset most impacted the church?

3. How do we navigate the tension of being a part of the world without resembling the world?

4. Read John 3:22-30. What does it look like for you to decrease and Jesus to increase? How do we seek this?

5. How does being eternally minded actually empower us to be of much earthly good? Give examples.

Close your time together in prayer

During the Next Week

1. Complete the two personal studies and evaluation.

2. Remind yourself daily that your citizenship is in heaven.

3. Take a look at your life and examine ways you resemble the world.

4. Memorize John 3:30.

Evaluation

Use the following questions to help you recognize
this mark of a disciple in your life.

How often do you consider God and what pleases Him in your daily life?

Do you find that you are more concerned about self-fulfillment or living a life
pleasing to God? Explain your answer.

How might the previous marks of a disciple we've studied—having a repentant life and healthy habits—help you focus your attention toward heaven?

Being eternally minded means that we eagerly anticipate the return of Christ. How often do you long for Christ to return? How might you incorporate this into your prayers this week?

Personal Study 1
CITIZENS OF HEAVEN

What does it mean to be a citizen of a country?

"Citizen" is one of those words we all think we understand but never really define. A citizen is simply a legally recognized resident of a particular place. In Philippians 3, Paul makes an incredible statement. He reminds the church in Philippi (and us today) that "our citizenship is in heaven" (v. 20). Remembering our true home in heaven is the essence of what it means to be eternally minded. It's living with the understanding that this life is not all there is. The author of Hebrews described Christians like this:

> For we do not have an enduring city here;
> instead, we seek the one to come.
> **HEBREWS 13:14**

Christians know that we don't have an enduring city here. Now, it's easy for Christians to nod and agree with that. It's a lot different to live that out. Our tendency is to want to make everything about here and now—how we feel, what we want, what others think, our status, our progression.

What are some ways you tend to focus on the here and now?

How does this keep you from focusing on your citizenship in heaven?

The letter to the Hebrews was written to persecuted believers who were struggling. The writer reminded them essentially, "this place is not your home. It will fade away. So instead of being overwhelmed by your circumstances here, focus your mind's attention and heart's affection on the city to come." That's a lot easier to practice when things are going poorly. When our lives are going well, we tend to feel at home in a place that was never supposed to feel like home. Instead of feeling at home, the Bible calls us to live as strangers and exiles.

Strangers and Exiles

Dear friends, I urge you as strangers and exiles to abstain
from sinful desires that wage war against the soul.
1 PETER 2:11

What is the difference between being an exile and a citizen?

How does the way Peter describes you as a Christian contrast with the way you see yourself?

Peter says every Christian should think of themselves as an exile. Some translations uses the words "sojourner," "foreigner," or "alien." As opposed to being a citizen, an exile is someone without a full-time legal status. Peter's original audience would've understood this metaphor immediately because of their Jewish heritage. In the Old Testament, God's people were taken from Israel and brought as exiles to Babylon. When they were in Babylon, they didn't consider themselves to be Babylonians, instead they were Jews living in Babylon. To put it in a modern context, Christians basically have a visa we carry around here on this earth and that visa will eventually expire and that is when Jesus will take us home.

**According to Peter, how should our exile status affect
the way we live and the choices we make?**

**How does this way of living stand in contrast to
the self-gratifying world we live in?**

Because we're strangers and exiles, we need to make sure that we don't become too comfortable with the customs of our temporary homes. Instead of embracing a way of life that is contrary to the Bible, we're to "abstain from sinful desires that wage war against the soul" (v. 11). Basically, Peter is saying a lot about this world is incompatible with our calling as Christians. While this world entices us to embrace our every desire, we should desire our eternal kingdom above all else (Matt. 6:33). But that doesn't mean we separate from the world. So what's the solution?

Conduct Yourselves Honorably

Conduct yourselves honorably among the Gentiles, so that
when they slander you as evildoers, they will observe your
good works and will glorify God on the day he visits.
1 PETER 2:12

**What does it look like to do good works in
the places God has called you?**

**How does doing good works cause people
to recognize your exile status?**

Believers aren't called to pull away from the world and hunker down in a holy huddle. We're exiles, but we're living among people. Instead of removing us from the world, God has left us here to be a redemptive presence in our communities so that people will see our good works and glorify God.

**What are some ways you can be a redemptive
presence in your community?**

God is most pleased when His children are confident that He is better than anything this world has to offer. That can only happen as we recognize our place as exiles and become so eternally minded, that we're of much earthly good.

In Closing

**Spend a few moments asking God to show you where
you can honor Him "among the Gentiles."**

**Next, ask Him to show you where you are too
comfortable living in this world and need to more
clearly embrace your citizenship in heaven.**

Personal Study 2
SEEK THE THINGS ABOVE

You've likely heard the old saying " be in the world, not of the world." As we've discussed throughout this session, this should be a reality for mature Christians. This mindset is a basic biblical concept, but grasping the implications of how this is carried out can be profound. Paul's letter to the Colossians helps us understand what it means to live it out.

Read Colossians 3:1-4.

What does it mean to be "raised with Christ?"

How should being raised with Christ affect every area of our lives?

To be raised with Christ means that our life and our identity are hidden with Him. We're secure in Him. We've been united with Him, and adopted into God's family. Because of our identity with Jesus, Paul tells us to "seek the things above" or in other words, "be heavenly minded." But why? Paul continues, "For you died," and that's what happens when we believe in Jesus. We die to who we used to be and the entire focus of our life shifts to who Christ wants for us to be. We've been forgiven of our sins. Now Jesus is the One who leads us. In the next few verses, Paul gives greater clarity to what that means.

Read Colossians 3:5-11.

Here Paul gave a list of behaviors and attitudes believers should avoid. Where do you see these in our culture?

Look at verses 7-8. What hope is available to those who are pursuing these things?

The Bible rarely, if ever, gives us rules for the sake of rules. The point of Scriptures is not, "Hey, knock that off." This is not about behavior; it's about worship. "It's about the heart," he says, which is idolatry. We worship other things instead of God, put things in the place of God. Because of this, we deserve the punishment of God for our sins, but thankfully by His love and grace, He punished Jesus in our place. Because of Jesus, these things describe who we once were, not who we now are (v. 7). Because of Jesus, we can put away these things and embrace the kind of eternally-minded life Christ calls us to (v. 8).

If we have the power to reject these sins, why do we sometimes fall into them?

Why does someone who believes in Jesus have a tendency to walk in sin? One of the main reasons why we drift back to who we used to be is we forget. We have a kind of functional walking amnesia where we forget that this world, as nice as it looks and as fun as it seems, is temporary. We forget there's only one world that endures forever and that is the kingdom of God. We forget partially because we're sinners with a sinful nature, but also because we live in a world where we're told to do whatever makes you happy which ironically, will never lead to happiness.

What is your thought pattern like when you find that you are falling into sin?

**Practically speaking, how can we actively seek
to set our mind on the things above?**

Because we're forgetful, we need to be reminded often that our hope is not in this world, but in heaven with Christ. We remember this hope through the Holy Spirit. We can only be eternally minded with His help. As we rely on the Spirit's help, we become more confident in our place as citizens of heaven and accept our identity as a people chosen and loved by God.

God's Chosen Ones, Holy and Dearly Loved

Read Colossians 3:12-17.

**How are the virtues described in this passage different
from the virtues the world embraces?**

**Look back to Colossians 3:1. Where are you setting
your mind every day? How does setting your mind
on Christ help you live these verses out?**

What would change if you realized your self-worth
was determined by the past, present, and future work
of Jesus Christ rather than your own work?

How does the body of Christ help us to be eternally minded?

All throughout this section of verses, Paul is pinning our ability to be eternally minded on Christ's work in us and our commitment to the church. Both are essential. We're exiles because Christianity will never be cool in our culture. To embrace countercultural values we need the support of our Savior and His life-transforming Spirit. We also need to participate in His body (the church) where we lock arms with other eternally minded people who say with us and with Jesus, "Your kingdom come. Your will be done on earth as it is in heaven (Matt. 6:10).

In Closing

What do you need to let go of in order to focus more fully on eternity?

Over the next week, how will you set your mind on the things above?

Marks of a Disciple

Session 4
GENEROUS LIVING

Start

Welcome to Session 4.

What challenged you from last session?
What encouraged you?

Last session we talked about how to be eternally minded and live as citizens of heaven. Being eternally minded encompasses all of life, including our finances which we'll talk about today.

What are some considerations you take into account when
making a budget for yourself or your family?

Being eternally minded is all about having our hearts in the right place. According to Jesus, one of the best ways to know where our hearts are is by how we spend our money (Matt. 6:21). Because our hearts matter to God and should matter to us, one of the ways we can measure Christian growth is through generosity.

Ask someone to pray, then watch the session 4 video together.

Watch

Use this space to take notes during the video teaching.

Discuss
Read Matthew 6:19-21 together.

> Don't store up for yourselves treasures on earth, where moth
> and rust destroy and where thieves break in and steal. But
> store up for yourselves treasures in heaven, where neither moth
> nor rust destroys, and where thieves don't break in and steal.
> For where your treasure is, there your heart will be also.
> **MATTHEW 6:19-21**

One of the ways God evaluates our hearts is by what we do with our resources. Disciples who are growing in their faith should be people of increasing generosity. We cannot serve God and money. Generosity allows us to keep our hearts in check.

1. How did Jesus link the way we spend our money to our hearts?

2. Why do we often miss the connection between our hearts and wallets?

3. Why is the act of giving as beneficial for the giver as it is for the ministry it funds? How has it matured you to give?

4. What are some ways we try to serve both God and money? What is the typical outcome when we do?

5. Based on this teaching, how would you describe the relationship Christians should have with their resources?

6. What are some ways we can be generous with what God has given us through our church and in our community?

Close your time together in prayer

During the Next Week

1. Complete the two personal studies and evaluation.

2. Make a simple budget that states how you plan to give to the Lord.

3. Look for ways you could invest in the kingdom of God.

4. Bless one person with your generosity this week.

5. Memorize Matthew 6:21.

Evaluation

Use the following questions to help you recognize this mark of a disciple in your life.

Generosity starts with giving 10 percent of your gross income to your local church through tithing. Do you tithe? If not, why not?

How generous are you with the resources God has entrusted to you? What do your finances reflect about your heart?

Are there areas in your monthly expenses that you could cut back on or do away with entirely to be more generous?

List a few ministries that you'd like to give to.

If you find it financially difficult to give, who could you consult about financial stewardship? What programs does your church offer?

Set a goal—either a percentage or an amount—to give this year. Write a plan below.

Personal Study 1

THE HEART OF GIVING

In his famous novel, *The Screwtape Letters*, author C. S. Lewis envisions an imaginary correspondence between two demons—the older Screwtape and his younger nephew Wormwood. Throughout the work, the older demon provides counsel to his nephew about how to impede the spiritual growth of a man known to the reading as "the patient." In one of the letters, Screwtape offers the following wisdom on prosperity:

> Prosperity knits a man to the World. He feels that he is "finding his place in it" while really it is finding its place in him. His increasing reputation, his widening circle of acquaintances, his sense of importance, the growing pressure of absorbing and agreeable work, build up in him a sense of being really at home in earth which is just what we want.[1]

How have you found these observations to be true in your own life and from what you've observed in the world around you?

How would you describe the way our culture feels about money and possessions?

Money and possessions are a deadly temptation for all of us because, as Lewis wrote, they "knit a man to the world." We cannot be eternally minded if we are constantly concerned with the things of earth. At every turn, our culture asks us to buy, consume, and dispose. We absorb these messages without thinking. They surround us at all times, seeking to make inroads to our hearts. Thankfully, Jesus was aware of the temptation that lurks for all of us in our possessions and He taught us a better way.

Where Your Heart Is

Read Matthew 6:19-21.

Why did Jesus caution against building up treasures on earth?

What does it look like to "store up treasures" in heaven?

What makes treasures in heaven more valuable than treasures on earth?

Why do we have a hard time seeing the difference?

In this teaching, Jesus gives straightforward wisdom that should be easy for all of us to pick up. Like Lewis did after Him, Jesus points out the temporary nature of possessions. Everything we own can be taken in an instant. By contrast, our treasures in heaven, the investment we make in the mission of God will never fade. So that leaves all of us with a choice: are we going to invest in the here and now or are we going to set our hearts and minds to eternity and invest in what can never be taken away.

How does money keep us from being eternally minded?

If Jesus taught that our treasure reveals our hearts, why
do we treat our possessions as a lesser concern?

Do we believe Jesus? Jesus teaches a great deal about money because He knows the way we use it signals where our heart is. In other words, our bank account shows us what we worship. If that's the case, we need to pay careful attention to how we spend the resources the Lord has given us, because we can only have one master.

One Master

Read Matthew 6:24.

The word Jesus uses for "serve" is the same word as "slave." How does
that help us understand what Jesus is teaching in this passage?

What does it look like when someone is enslaved by their money?

The word Jesus frequently used for servant has the same root word as "serve." They both describe a relationship of a bondservant and a master. In other words, there is not an equal partnership. Either we are mastered by Jesus or mastered by our possessions. Jesus is emphatic that there is no middle ground.

What changes about generosity when you see it the way Jesus sees it?

**Why might this mark of a disciple be harder
for us to embrace than others?**

**What changes do you need to make to ensure that you
are not being mastered by your possessions?**

In Closing

Spend a few moments in prayer evaluating what you treasure.
Ask how you might reinvest in the kingdom of God.

[1] C. S. Lewis, *The Screwtape Letters* (New York, NY: HarperOne, 1942).

Personal Study 2

GIVING AS DISCIPLINE

In the previous personal study we examined giving as a measurement of our hearts toward God. In this personal study, we're going to look at generosity as a matter of spiritual discipline. Matters of discipline are not unrelated to the heart. Take Bible reading, for example. We love God so we want to hear from Him through His Word. However, to regularly hear from God takes discipline. So it is with generosity. To be generous, we must be diligent and intentional.

Why should we consider generosity a spiritual discipline as well as a posture of the heart?

Excel in this Act of Grace

Read 2 Corinthians 8:1-9.

In 1 Corinthians 16:1-4 Paul appealed to the Corinthian church asking them for help with a financial collection for the church in Jerusalem. Apparently the Corinthians agreed to give, but then never participated. In 2 Corinthians 8–9, Paul directs the Corinthian church about how to steward their resources.

What had the Macedonian church done?

What do the Macedonians teach us about the nature of generosity?

Paul pointed out the Macedonian church as an example because they gave when it was difficult. They were not well off, and yet, they gave beyond their means. For them, generosity was gift of grace that God had given them to share with people who needed it. Paul encouraged the Corinthians to give with the same degree of generosity.

What does it look like for you to "excel" in the grace of giving?

Paul didn't specify a set amount or percentage for their giving. What does this teach us?

Glance back at verse 9. Upon what did Paul base the desire to give?

Those who have been dealt the most generously should be the most generous with their time, resources, influence, and compassion. And let's be honest, no one has been dealt with more generously than people who can claim the name of Christ. We are people who were dead in our sins and made alive. Our greatest need has already been met, we were separated from God, and now we've been reconciled to Him by the blood of Christ. Through the Scriptures, God is telling us that because of Christ's sacrifice, we should sacrifice for others.

How does the gospel compel your giving?

Practical Generosity

Understanding the basis for giving, let's examine what generosity looks like in practice.

How do we balance being grateful and guilty for the blessings we have been given?

Read 1 Timothy 6:10. How is this passage often taken out of context?

The Bible never calls to feel guilty for having an abundance. How much we make is never the issue, rather it's how much we give. To "excel" in giving means to leverage your resources for the kingdom of God. When we ask "How much do I give?," we're still not asking the right questions. Don't think abstractly about it. "This is how much we owe God this year." Don't think that way. Rather, think about it in this manner. using the following questions.

How is God using my resources to do a work in me?

How is God using my resources to do a work for others?

Like everything else in the kingdom of God, our generosity should show our love for God and love for others. That's the heart aspect of it. However, for generosity to be a spiritual discipline, it needs to be planned to be done well. This begins with a tithe (giving 10 percent of your gross income to your church), and it extends beyond ten percent in love of God and others.

Beyond your tithe, where is an area through your church or in your city that you would like to see the Lord work? How much could you give to support that work?

Is there a cause of felt need you feel passionately about? What would it look like to support this cause with your finances?

Thinking beyond finances, what other resources—time, talents, non-financial gifts—do you have at your disposal? Where can you use those to serve God and others?

In Closing

Who is the most generous Christian you know? What could you learn about giving from observing their life?

Marks of a Disciple

Session 5

THEOLOGICALLY SOUND

Start
Welcome to Session 5.

Last session we thought about what it means to be generous stewards of all that God has entrusted to us. This session we're going to focus on our desire to know God and live in accordance with our beliefs.

How did last session challenge you to live more generously?

This session is about what it means to be theologically sound. Studying theology is not just something pastors and people in seminary do, it's something all of us do as we think about God and live according to our beliefs about God. A growing disciple will always be increasing in their love for and knowledge of God.

Outside of the Bible, what is one resource that has helped you grow as a Christian?

What was helpful about it?

Ask someone to pray, then watch the session 5 video together.

Watch

Use this space to take notes during the video teaching.

Discuss
Read Hebrews 1:1-2 together.

> Long ago God spoke to our ancestors by the prophets at
> different times and in different ways. In these last days, he
> has spoken to us by his Son. God has appointed him heir
> of all things and made the universe through him.
>
> **HEBREWS 1:1-2**

Theology is important because it unites the church around the truth of God's Word. Being theologically sound doesn't mean we have all the information we need to ace Bible trivia, but rather that we know and apply the Scriptures correctly.

1. According to Hebrews, God has spoken to us through His Word. What responsibility do we have to know Him through His Word?

2. What are some ways we discount or downplay this mark of a disciple?

3. Though doctrine is seen by some as divisive, why is doctrine actually unifying? What is the danger of having bad theology?

4. Why is it insufficient to simply say, "Love God, and love people"? Why do we need to be more specific?

5. What is theological triage? How does this help us understand which beliefs and doctrines matter most?

6. Beyond reading the Bible, what are some ways we can seek to be theologically sound?

Close your time together in prayer

During the Next Week

1. Complete the two personal studies and evaluation.

2. Spend time over the next five days reading the Bible for 10 minutes.

3. Ask a pastor or trusted friend for a Christian book recommendation.

4. Memorize Hebrews 1:1-2.

Evaluation

Use the following questions to help you recognize
this mark of a disciple in your life.

Dean shared that what comes to mind when you think about God is the most
important thing about you. So what comes to your mind when you think
about God?

"Theology" is literally the study of God. How are you seeking to know God by
knowing theology?

On the other hand, knowing theology should never cause us to be unloving.
Being unloving reflects a lack of knowledge about God. Has your theological
knowledge ever led you to become prideful? Explain.

How might developing a right understanding of theological triage lead us to study theology with humility and love?

If you feel that this is an area you can grow, who might be able to disciple or mentor you? When will you reach out to them?

Personal Study 1

HOLD FAST TO TRUTH

Everyone thinks about God. To go one step further, everyone believes something about God. Even one who claims there is no god, believes something about God—namely that He doesn't exist. Therefore, everyone is a theologian. Pastor A. W. Tozer famously said:

> What comes to mind when we think about God is the most important thing about us.[1]

Tozer pointed out that what we believe about God is of great consequence. Being theologically sound is a mark of a growing disciple because it means we are seeking to know the One true God, truly, as He exists, not as we would like for Him to be. The goal of reading and teaching Scripture is to love God, not to be right. Because God has spoken, we have a responsibility to know Him. Theology is simply knowing God as He has revealed Himself in His Word. When we know God through His Word, we begin to pursue lives that please Him. Christian doctrine answers two questions: *Who is God?* and *Why does that matter?*

Who is God?

Most of the New Testament letters were written to instruct believers and correct false teaching. Paul did this regularly. As he went on missionary journeys he planted churches and raised up elders to lead to those churches. Paul frequently used his letters to encourage good theology and correct false teaching. He often did both in the same letter because our theology shapes the way we live. In Titus, Paul called the leaders of the church to help the church to train the body in sound doctrine.

Read Titus 1:5-9.

Why did Paul leave Titus behind in Crete?

What role do elders (or pastors) have in helping
the church become theologically sound?

Take a closer look at verse 9. What does it mean to
hold to the faithful message? According to Paul,
what does holding on to truth allow us to do?

Titus is a letter written to a young pastor about how about how the church should function. While this passage describes the role of pastors or elders in the church, it is applicable to all of us. Out of the gate Paul focused on the importance of being theologically sound. He's not saying, "Hey, how you doing?" He's saying we need to make sure we get this stuff right because everything hinges on it. He argued faithful instruction in the truth is needed to encourage the church and refute false gospels our culture preaches to us.

Where else in the New Testament do we see
instruction to correct false teaching?

If correcting false teaching is such a priority in the New Testament, why
should we make being theologically sound a priority in our own lives?

Having sound doctrine is a repeated theme throughout the New Testament. Paul opposed false teaching almost more than anything else. He wasn't concerned with having correct theology to win arguments but rather so that we can reach the world. So we can reach our neighbors and show them there's a better way. They can stop buying the lie that they need to go around God, not to Him for meaning and satisfaction and fulfillment. All of us are called to "contend for the faith that was delivered to the saints once for all" (Jude 3). We contend for the truth because we can only truly understand ourselves once we understand God.

How Should We Live?

Read Titus 2:1–15.

Titus 2 begins with the statement "But you are to proclaim things consistent with sound teaching" (v. 1). Everything after that statement flows from it. Paul is saying, once we understand theology, it should impact the way we live. The Books of Romans and Ephesians are organized this way. The first half of these books center on theology and the second half examines how we should live in light of sound teaching.

According to this chapter in Titus, how does sound teaching shape the way we live?

What categories of people does this chapter address? What are some specific takeaways for you?

What are some ways faulty theology might impact the way you live?

Our theology matters. Our beliefs determine how we respond in tragedy and how we respond when things are going fantastic. Theology determines how we view our money, relationships, marriage, choices, and parenting. We approach all of these things by what comes to our mind when we think about God. Being theologically sound matters because it answers the most essential questions of our lives.

How might having a poor theology lead us to make choices that aren't honoring to God?

How have your beliefs about God shaped the decisions that you make?

Everyone has an answer to the question, "What comes to your mind when you think about God?" It might take you a couple of minutes to form that in our minds, but each of us has an answer. We're all theologians. The question is, does your theology agree with God's self-revelation in Scripture, and how does that theology shape the way you live?

In Closing

Spend a few moments considering ways you need to adjust your decisions and conduct as a result of something you've studied in Scripture.

[1.] A. W. Tozer, *The Knowledge of the Holy: the Attributes of God* (San Francisco, Ca.: HarperSanFrancisco, 1992).

Personal Study 2

TRUTH IN PRACTICE

In the previous personal study we looked at two central questions our theology answers: *Who is God?* and *Why does that matter?* We used words like "theology," "doctrine," "belief," and "truth." All these terms refer to the same object—Jesus. Consider what Jesus said about Himself.

> I am the way, the truth, and the life. No one
> comes to the Father except through me.
> **JOHN 14:6**

What implications does Jesus' statement have for our commitment to sound theology?

Jesus claimed that He was the embodiment of truth. He believed and taught that all of Scripture pointed to Him (John 5:39). Sound theology matters because knowing Jesus matters, and we can only know Jesus truly by having sound theology. Doctrine is not a matter of secondary importance but rather it is the center of our faith. This doesn't mean that we have everything figured out. It does mean we have a desire to grow in our understanding of central Christian beliefs. Before He went to the cross, Jesus prayed that His church would unified in the truth.

Jesus' Prayer

Read John 17:17–23.

According to Jesus' prayer, why should truth unify the church?

Based on these verses, how might you respond to someone who believed theology was a matter of secondary importance?

What are some ways that doctrine and theology unify the church?

In these verses, Jesus is saying the point of having the truth is unity. Truth is the organizing principle behind Christianity. We believe in the truth about Jesus and that truth knits us together in Him. In Jesus we are one as the Father, Son, and Spirit are one. Embracing the truth means embracing God Himself. In the Scriptures, it is always those who step away from truth that cause division. Unity never exists for the sake of unity. We have to be unified around something or someone. Jesus prayed that we would be unified around Him, and He is the truth. Sound theology unifies and sanctifies.

What does it mean to be sanctified in the truth?

How has studying theology lead to your growth as a disciple of Jesus?

Truth is sanctifying because it grows our love and commitment to Jesus. Unity and theology go together. As we grow in our love for Jesus, we will naturally gravitate toward others as our love for Jesus is built up together. Based on our love for the truth, Jesus sends us into the world to teach others about Him. Theology drives mission.

How does our theology inform our commitment to mission?

In the Great Commission, Jesus commanded us to teach others to observe all that He commanded (Matt. 28:19-20). In His prayer in John 17, Jesus prayed that we would be sanctified in the truth right before He acknowledged that He was sending us into the world. Mission arises from a commitment to sound theology. But that leads us to an important question: *How do we recognize sound theology?*

How do I Recognize Sound Teaching?

In order to grow in our understanding of doctrine, we have to be able to recognize sound teaching. Here are five questions we can ask of any teaching we encounter to verify whether or not that teaching is theologically sound.

1. What does the Bible actually say in context?

This is the most important question to ask of any teaching. Sound theology is rarely developed from quoting isolated verses. Rather, we need to consider Scripture in context. Sure, we might be able to pull teaching from verse 11, and it might sound good and be an awesome post with flowers behind it on social media, but we need to see what verses 9, 10, 12, and 13 say. We need to seek to understand what this verse meant to the original audience.

2. Is this a consistent teaching of the Scriptures throughout church history?

There's a saying that goes, "If it's true, it's probably not new and if it's new, it's probably not true." While Scripture is the final word, we can also learn from how the church has historically interpreted the Scriptures. When developing our theological convictions, we need to consider the witness of the church. We need to ask, what has the historic church taught about an issue throughout the past 2,000 years?

3. Do I have to twist the Scriptures to fit my position?

Our positions should come from Scripture instead of the other way around. All Scripture has a context and context helps us understand meaning. When we take Scripture out of context, we're doing what is called proof-texting and twisting Scripture to mean something other than what it has always meant.

4. Am I being promised things that God doesn't actually promise?

We see this error often when people are going through a difficult time and a well-meaning friend says something like "God will never give you more than you can handle." That sentiment sounds good and even spiritual, but Scripture doesn't teach that. In fact, if God never gave us more than we could handle, there would be no need to rely on Him.

5. Is this true in any time or place in history?

Scripture is true at all places and all times because Scripture reveals God's unchanging character. Therefore, when we're seeking to apply Scripture, the principles we observe from Scripture should be ones that are true in any place and at any time in history.

Of these questions, which one is most helpful to you, and why?

**What, if any, theological convictions do you need
to reevaluate in response to these questions?**

In Closing

**Thank God for giving us the ability to know Him. Pray that
you would seek to grow in your knowledge of Him.**

Marks of a Disciple

Session 6
MISSIONAL HEART

Start
Welcome to Session 6.

Last session we studied the importance of being theologically sound. In this final session, we're going a step further and talk about how growing disciples are increasingly motivated by a missional heart.

Look back at the five questions on pages 86-87.
Which was most helpful to you and why?

As we said last session, our theology should affect the way we live. This should be most evident in our heart toward people who don't yet know Jesus. We're the most like Jesus when we're following Him into the world. So in this last session of study, we're going to see what it means to have a missional heart.

What excites you about being on mission with Jesus?

What, if any, hesitations do you have following Jesus into mission?

Ask someone to pray, then watch the session 6 video together.

Watch

Use this space to take notes during the video teaching.

Discuss
Read Luke 19:10 together.

> For the Son of Man has come to seek and to save the lost.
>
> **LUKE 19:10**

When we think of Christian maturity, we often hear about spiritual practices like Bible reading, prayer, and giving, but we don't often hear about someone who has a heart for the lost. We are never more like Jesus than when we are seeking our lost friends, so having a missional heart is an essential mark of a growing disciple.

1. How did Jesus model reaching out to people who were far from God? What can we learn from His example?

2. Why don't we make seeking the lost as much of a priority as Jesus did?

3. Why is it important to connect with lost friends on their terms and on their turf? Why might this be better than inviting them to church?

4. What are some ways that you can connect to people who are far from God in your community?

5. Dean began by sharing the story of a college student in the church he pastors who made time for lost friends. Where could you make space to spend time with your lost friends?

6. What is you most significant takeaway from the past six sessions?

Close your time together in prayer

During the Next Week

1. Complete the two personal studies and evaluation.

2. Intentionally pray for one lost friend.

3. Write out your own gospel story to help you share it with others.

4. Actively look for opportunities to tell someone about Jesus.

5. Memorize Luke 19:10

6. Complete the final evaluation on pages 104–105.

Evaluation
Use the following questions to help you recognize
this mark of a disciple in your life.

How many friends do you have outside of church circles? How often are you
praying for and seeking opportunities to share Jesus with them?

What hesitations do you have about being on mission with Jesus? Be honest.
Write out your struggles, and ask for help overcoming your hesitations.

What talents, hobbies, or interests has God given you that might help you connect with people who don't know Jesus?

List the names of 3-5 lost friends, coworkers, family members, or neighbors. Spend intentional time over the next week asking for God to open their hearts to the gospel and to give you the opportunity to share with them.

Personal Study 1

SEEK AND SAVE

Throughout the Gospel of Luke, Jesus intentionally spends time with the lost and down-trodden. He spends time with Gentiles. He frequently dines with tax collectors and sinners. Said another way, He makes space in His life for people who do not know God. In chapter 19, Jesus tells us why He organized His life this way:

For the Son of Man has come to seek and to save the lost.
LUKE 19:10

Rephrase Jesus' mission in your own words.

How would you define your mission as a follow of Jesus?

Jesus didn't come to be a great teacher, and He didn't come to be a great healer, though He was both of those things. Jesus came to seek and to save the lost. The simple, straightforward, unadorned mission of Jesus was to save lost sinners. For us to be growing disciples, Jesus' mission has to become our mission. However, we have often settled for less.

Our Mission

All of us have different gifts and callings that God expects us to use. Some of us are called to serve in vocational ministry working in churches and ministries. Others of us have been called to the marketplace as accountants, managers, or other kinds of skilled workers. Others still may be called for a time or a lifetime to serve in the home. Some reading may have entered into retirement.

Describe your stage of life. Where has God called you to serve?

**How does this stage give you unique opportunities
to be on mission with Jesus?**

We all have the same mission—to join Jesus in His mission to seek and save the lost. This mission has two components than we need to pursue—seeking and saving.

Seeking

Seeking is Jesus' posture toward lost people. In Luke 7, Jesus described how His critics saw Him.

> The Son of Man has come eating and drinking, and you say, "Look,
> a glutton and a drunkard, a friend of tax collectors and sinners!"
> **LUKE 7:34**

What do these verses tell us about Jesus' relationship with lost people?

Jesus welcomed people who did not know Him. They saw Him as their friend. Tax collectors and sinners—people who were outcast and thought to be far from God—wanted to have dinner with Him. They wouldn't have come to Him unless they felt welcome with Him. Yet, in many of our Christian circles, it's easy to neglect outside friendships and only spend time with Christian friends. Spending time with other people who know and love Jesus is natural and commanded in Scripture, but we shouldn't limit our friendships to those who are only Christians. To do that would also be ignoring Scripture.

How would you characterize your relationship with lost people?

What are a few ways you can make time and space in your life to welcome and befriend the "tax collectors and sinners" around you?

Our mission starts with befriending and seeking lost people, but it cannot stop there. Jesus spent time with and enjoyed being around lost people, but He also came to save.

Saving

Jesus came to save, but from what exactly? From the penalty of sin. We can seek lost people, but we cannot save them. The power to save belongs to Jesus alone. We participate in the mission of Jesus by connecting with lost friends and sharing the hope of the gospel with them.

How would you summarize the gospel message?

The gospel message is that God is a Holy God and we have rebelled against Him. He made us to be in a relationship with Him. But we have all said, "God, no thanks. I don't want you. I want your stuff instead. I don't want your way. I want my way." God being a holy God can't let sin go unpunished. So Jesus came to take the punishment for our sins—to seek and to save those who are lost through His death on the cross. Through the cross, three things happened. One, the people of God would be saved, the justice of God would be satisfied, and the love of God would be revealed. We are never more like Jesus than when we are taking this message to our lost friends.

If having a heart for the lost is the essence of what it means to follow Jesus, why do we elevate other things above spreading the gospel?

Think back to the question of calling on the last page. How can you share the gospel with the people who you naturally interact with?

If discipleship and growing in our faith means becoming more like Christ, having a heart for the lost is at the center of what it means to follow Jesus. It is the cause Jesus devoted His life to and the mission He died for. We are never more like Jesus than when we follow Him into the world.

In Closing

How might you need to adjust your mission to more closely align with Jesus' mission?

Spend some time today asking Jesus where you can join Him in His work of seeking and saving the lost.

Personal Study 2
JESUS' LOVE FOR THE LOST

In the previous personal study we took a look at Jesus' primary motivation to seek and save the lost. In this personal study, we're going to look at Jesus' love for the lost.

If saving the lost was Jesus' primary mission, why is it rarely at the center of what we consider it means to be a Christian?

For some reason, having a missional heart not a very popular description of what it means to be like Christ. But Jesus never wavered on His mission and He even had to answer for it regularly.

Jesus and Complainers

Read Luke 15:1-2.

Notice that "tax collectors and sinners" approached Jesus (v. 1) and were welcomed by Him (v. 2). What made people far from God comfortable around Jesus?

Who were the Pharisees and scribes? What made them so incensed about the company Jesus kept?

In Luke 15, he tells a story to prove a point. The scene is set for us that all the tax collectors and sinners were approaching to listen to him. First century tax collectors were kind of a reverse Robin Hood. They would actually prey on the poor because they had authority from Rome to levy taxes on the Jewish people and often took advantage of that ability by taking more than they were owed. It's interesting that this audience wanted to hear what Jesus had to say. On the other hand, the most religious people—the Pharisees and scribes—were infuriated by Jesus' proximity to sinners. They reasoned, "if He's the Messiah, He shouldn't be focused on those folks at all because they're unclean, they're sinners." In their complaints, they missed the heart of Christ.

Why do many "religious people" today distance themselves from sinners?

Why is the desire to distance actually counterproductive to our mission?

Jesus' mission was often misunderstood by the Jewish religious teachers who should've understood it immediately. To help them understand, Jesus told a parable to explain His love for the lost.

Jesus and the Lost

Read Luke 15:3-7.

What does the shepherd in this story do that lets you know he cares about the sheep?

What would motivate a shepherd to leave 99 sheep to find one?

Jesus lived in an agrarian society so this story would've been a familiar scenario for His audience. The problem for us a couple of thousand years later, is this doesn't seem like business sense? If you are a shepherd, leaving 99 sheep to find one doesn't seem to make a lot of sense, unless you consider the heart of the shepherd. The shepherd knew the sheep, he cared for them day after day. He had an affection for his sheep that drove him to prioritize the one who was lost over the 99 who were safe at home.

How did the shepherd react when he returned home with the sheep?

What does this parable teach us about the heart of Christ?

In this parable, Jesus was saying to the Pharisees and scribes—and to us today—why He cares for the lost. It's because there's sheep without a shepherd. They're sheep without a shepherd and in this moment, you are looking into the heart of the shepherd. The angels are going to party more over one person coming to Christ than they are anything else. Notice what he doesn't say, "Don't you know that the heavens rejoice over somebody having an awesome Bible study?" Those are important and I do think angels care about this, but that doesn't start a party in heaven. The joy of heaven and the heart of the Savior are full when lost sinners come home to the Shepherd.

If that's the cause for celebration in heaven, how should that influence and shape our churches?

On the other hand, what does it say about us if our hearts are unmoved and unmotivated by care for lost people?

Having a missional heart is an essential marker of a growing disciple. Our concern cannot simply be for our own spiritual health and our own growth. The most basic definition of a disciple is "a learner." To be an effective disciple, we should increasingly become more like our teacher. Our teacher cares deeply for the lost. He loves them so much that He came to earth to save them. He has done it for you and longs to do it for others as well.

In Closing

What would change about your heart for the lost if you spent the next week praying for those in your life by name every day?

What is you biggest takeaway from this week of study?

Final Evaluation

Use the following questions to look back at what you learned and look forward to further growth.

Repentant Life

How have you grown in this area?

How will you continue to grow?

Healthy Habits

How have you grown in this area?

How will you continue to grow?

Eternally Minded

How have you grown in this area?

How will you continue to grow?

Theologically Sound

How have you grown in this area?

How will you continue to grow?

Generous Living

How have you grown in this area?

How will you continue to grow?

Missional Heart

How have you grown in this area?

How will you continue to grow?

MARKS
of a
DISCIPLE

|ılıılıılıılıılıılıılıılıılıılıılıılıılıılıılıılıılıılıılıılıılıılıılı|

Six Measurements for Growth

|ıllıllıllıllıllıllıllıllıllıllıllıllıllıllıllıllıllıllıllıllıllıllıllıll|

Dean Inserra

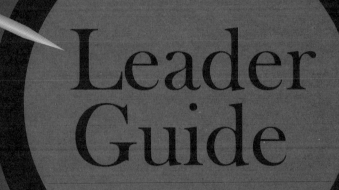

HOW TO USE THE LEADER GUIDE

Prepare to Lead

Each leader guided is designed to be cut out so that you, the leader, can keep this front-and-back page with you as you lead the group session.

Watch the session's teaching video and read the group content with the leader guide tear-out in hand to understand how it supplements each section of the group study.

Mark Defined

This section summarizes the mark of a disciple that will be studied for each session.

Key Scriptures

A quick reference guide for Scriptures used in the session as well as the personal studies.

Considerations

Because most people have experience with singleness, dating, engagement, and marriage, this section alerts you to some of the assumptions members may bring with them to the group sessions.

Questions to Consider

This section contains a few questions to send to group members during the week to foster connection and engagement in between group meetings.

Notes

Use this section to record any thoughts or notes that you have.

TIPS FOR LEADING A SMALL GROUP

Follow these guidelines to prepare for each group session.

Prayerfully Prepare

REVIEW. Review the weekly material and group questions ahead of time.

PRAY. Be intentional about praying for each person in the group.

Ask the Holy Spirit to work through you and the group discussion as you point to Jesus each week through God's Word.

Minimize Distractions

Create a comfortable environment. If group members are uncomfortable, they'll be distracted and therefore not engaged in the group experience. Plan ahead by considering these details, include seating, temperature, lighting, food and drink, and general cleanliness. Do everything in your ability to help people focus on what's most important: connecting with God, with the Bible, and with one another.

Encourage Discussion

A good small-group experience has the following characteristics.

EVERYONE IS INCLUDED. Your goal is to foster a community in which people are welcome just as they are but encouraged to grow spiritually. Always be aware of opportunities to include any people who visit the group and to invite new people to join your group.

EVERYONE PARTICIPATES. Encourage everyone to ask questions, share responses, or read aloud.

NO ONE DOMINATES—NOT EVEN THE LEADER. Be sure that your time speaking as a leader takes up less than half of your time together as a group. Politely guide discussion if anyone dominates.

NOBODY IS RUSHED THROUGH QUESTIONS. Don't feel that a moment of silence is a bad thing. People often need time to think about their responses to questions they've just heard or to gain courage to share what God is stirring in their hearts.

INPUT IS AFFIRMED AND FOLLOWED UP. Make sure you point out something true or helpful in a response. Don't just move on. Build community with follow-up questions, asking how other people have experienced similar things or how a truth has shaped their understanding of God and the Scripture you're studying. People are less likely to speak up if they fear that you don't actually want to hear their answers or that you're looking for only a certain answer.

GOD AND HIS WORD ARE CENTRAL. Opinions and experiences can be helpful, but God has given us the truth. Trust God's Word to be the authority and God's Spirit to work in people's lives. You can't change anyone, but God can. Continually point people to the Word and to active steps of faith.

Keep Connecting

Think of ways to connect with group members during the week. Participation during the group session is always improved when members spend time connecting with one another outside the group sessions. The more people are comfortable with and involved in one another's lives, the more they'll look forward to being together. When people move beyond being friendly to truly being friends who form a community, they come to each session eager to engage instead of merely attending.

Encourage group members with thoughts, commitments, or questions from the session by connecting through these communication channels:

EMAILS

TEXTS

SOCIAL MEDIA

When possible, build deeper friendships by planning or spontaneously inviting group members to join you outside your regularly scheduled group time for activities like these:

MEALS

FUN ACTIVITIES

PROJECTS AROUND YOUR HOME, CHURCH, OR COMMUNITY

Session 1
REPENTANT LIFE

Mark Defined

While we are fully forgiven from our sins the moment we believe the gospel, we continue to sin in our walk with the Lord and need to seek forgiveness and restoration. Simply put, repentance is our response to God's goodness, kindness, and grace in our lives. Disciples of Jesus Christ should be characterized by a lifestyle of repentance.

Key Scriptures

Romans 2:4 // Genesis 3:1-7// Ephesians 3:4-9 // Psalm 139:23-24 // Romans 12:1-2

Considerations

Many in your group may have never considered repentance in the way it is described in this session. As the leader you want to be sensitive to this and helpful as they see a difficult topic in a new way.

Remember repentance doesn't come naturally to any of us. However, as we understand the gravity of sin, we begin to understand the grace of repentance.

Help the group understand they are already fully forgiven by God. Their initial act of repentance was accepted and effective, however ongoing repentance brings intimacy with God and others as our hearts learn to abstain from sin and embrace Jesus daily.

Questions to Consider

How has this session shifted your perspective on repentance?

Set aside time each day to examine your heart and repent to God or others. After you've done this practice for a couple of days, see what has changed about your heart toward God.

Notes

....

....

....

....

....

....

....

....

....

....

....

....

....

....

....

....

....

....

....

....

Session 2
HEALTHY HABITS

Mark Defined

We maintain our physical health through regular habits like diet, exercise, staying hydrated, and being well-rested. We maintain our spiritual health by engaging in spiritual habits like Bible reading, prayer, and serving in a local church. While these are by no means the only spiritual disciplines, focusing on these three habits will set you on a path to enduring spiritual health.

Key Scriptures

2 Peter 3:18 // 2 Timothy 3:16-17 // Acts 2:42-47; 20:28

Considerations

Some in your group will have a history of spiritual disciplines while others have never established a healthy rhythm. Do your best to encourage people wherever they are.

Stress that how much we read the Bible, pray, and participate in the life of a church doesn't save us or make us more acceptable to God, only the gospel does that.

Many people give up these habits when they miss or feel like they can't get on track. It's better to start back or get back on board than to continue not participating out of guilt.

Some will not see the need for church membership. Try to discern what their objections may be, and stress that this idea is assumed in the New Testament.

Questions to Consider

What is God teaching you through your Bible reading this week?

How can I pray for you?

What is one way you can contribute to the life and health of our church this week?

Notes

....
....
....
....
....
....
....
....
....
....
....
....
....
....
....
....
....
....
....

Session 3
ETERNALLY MINDED

Mark Defined

We are naturally bent to consider ourselves first, while we generally agree this isn't good, we are less inclined to agree on a solution. The solution is to be eternally minded. To be eternally minded is to give Jesus the first consideration in your heart and life. It's obeying the command to love God with your heart, mind, and strength, and love your neighbor as yourself.

Key Scriptures

Philippians 3:18-20 // Hebrews 13:4 // 1 Peter 2:11-12; Colossians 3:1-17

Considerations

Keep in mind that we are all naturally self-centered. Becoming eternally minded will be a process for all of us.

Press into the analogy of being citizens of heaven. Once we shift our thinking away from the here and now, we begin to see matters of eternal significance more clearly.

The message of this session stands in stark contrast to the self-fulfillment message seen everywhere in our culture. Encourage people to see how they've been impacted by this teaching and adjust their thinking.

Questions to Consider

Examine the ways your life has been impacted by the gospel of self-fulfillment that is constantly preached in our culture.

How is the life and heart of Jesus increasing in your life this week? How does that naturally lead you away from the desire for self-fulfillment?

Notes

....

....

....

....

....

....

....

....

....

....

....

....

....

....

....

....

....

....

....

....

....

Session 4
GENEROUS LIVING

Mark Defined

Growing disciples should be marked by growing generosity. When our hearts are right with God it drives us to be generous with all the gifts that God has given us.

Key Scriptures

Matthew 6:19-21 // 2 Corinthians 8:1-9

Considerations

Money and giving may be difficult to talk about, but Jesus said how we spend our money reveals our hearts. To ignore and never talk about our finances is to ignore our hearts.

Many people do not give to the local church. If you discover this is the case in your group, seek to find out why. It's usually because of financial or spiritual hardship—either way this should be addressed. Seek the wisdom of a pastor or trusted leader if you feel ill-equipped for these kinds of conversations.

Encourage people to give beyond the tithe and beyond their finances. We can also give of our time and talents.

Questions to Consider

What is an expense you could eliminate or reduce in your budget to give more to God's Work in the world?

What breaks your heart about the world? What Christian organizations are addressing this need? Do some research, then pray and ask God where He would have you give to this cause and these organizations.

Notes

....

....

....

....

....

....

....

....

....

....

....

....

....

....

....

....

....

....

Session 5
THEOLOGICALLY SOUND

Mark Defined

What comes to our minds when we think about God is the most important thing about us. Theology may seem intimidating to us, but theology is simply the study of God. Being theologically sound means we desire to know the true God truly.

Key Scriptures

Hebrews 1:1-2 // Titus 1:5-9; 2:1-15 // John 17:17-23

Considerations

Some may see theology as something for pastors or super Christians, but in reality, theology is for all of us. Each of us practice theology because each of us thinks about God.

Some may have been in churches that split over theology. This is not the point of theology. True theology should always be a point of unity and not division.

This session is not about making sure everyone believes the right things, but rather it aims to help us begin thinking about theology and its importance for the Christian life.

Questions to Consider

What shapes your view of God?

How does your view of God shape every other aspect of your life?

Notes

....

....

....

....

....

....

....

....

....

....

....

....

....

....

....

....

....

....

....

Session 6
MISSIONAL HEART

Mark Defined

Jesus came to earth to seek and save the lost. We're the most like Jesus when we're following Him into the world to tell everyone the good news of the gospel. Being a disciple comes with the calling to go and make disciples of all nations.

Key Scriptures

Luke 15:3-7; 19:10

Considerations

Sharing the gospel intimidates many people. Some people in your group may have never shared the gospel with another person, even if they've been a Christian for many years. The goal here is not to make them feel bad, but rather to help them see this as a crucial aspect of the Christian life.

Link the advance of the gospel to Jesus' purpose in coming to earth. We all like to define Jesus by our own standards, but if we examine what Jesus actually cared about, we'll see His mission to the lost was the front edge of all He did.

Help people see that having a heart for the lost begins with having lost friends. Jesus loved lost people and spent a lot of time with them. We can too—not as a project but as friends. This is an easy first step into developing a missional heart.

Questions to Consider

Where can you spend time around lost friends?

What adjustments need to be made to your schedule to be around lost people?

Notes

....

....

....

....

....

....

....

....

....

....

....

....

....

....

....

....

....

....

....

MORE FROM
Lifeway adults

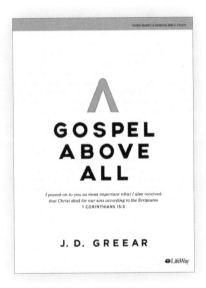

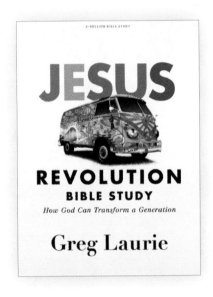

GOSPEL ABOVE ALL
J.D. Greear

See that the impetus for the church's
ministry is not a new strategy or an
updated message but a return to
elevating the gospel above all.
(8 sessions)

Leader Kit 005814259 **$99.99**
Bible Study Book 005814001 **$14.99**

lifeway.com/gospelaboveall

JESUS REVOLUTION
How God Can Transform a Generation
Greg Laurie

Discover a reason to believe the next
great American revival may be on its
way. (6 sessions)

Leader Kit 005823248 **$89.99**
Bible Study Book 005823247 **$14.99**

lifeway.com/jesusrevolution

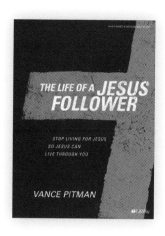

THE LIFE OF A JESUS FOLLOWER
**Stop Living for Jesus so Jesus
Can Live Through You**
Vance Pitman

Walk away from the "burden" of religion and
discover the purity and simplicity of following
Jesus. (8 sessions)

Leader Kit 005815995 **$79.99**
Bible Study Book 005815993 **$14.99**

lifeway.com/jesusfollower

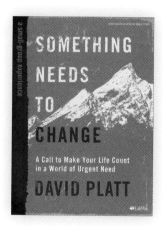

SOMETHING NEEDS TO CHANGE
**A Call to Make Your Life Count
in a World of Urgent Need**
David Platt

Be inspired to respond to spiritual and physical
needs with urgency and Christlike compassion.
(8 sessions)

Leader Kit 005816664 **$79.99**
Bible Study Book 005802005 **$14.99**

lifeway.com/somethingneedstochange

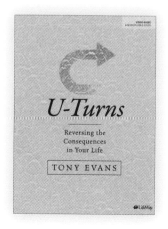

U-TURNS
Reversing the Consequences in Your Life
Tony Evans

Learn to align your life choices under God's Word
and change the direction of your life. (6 sessions)

Leader Kit 005803942 **$99.99**
Bible Study Book 005803941 **$14.99**

lifeway.com/uturns

ORDER ONLINE OR CALL 800.458.2772.

Prices and availability subject to change without notice.

Are you growing in your faith?

Every Christian is designed by God to grow in faith. But how do you follow Jesus really? What does Jesus say about following Him? How can you know if you're doing okay?

Marks of a Disciple offers helpful targets to aim for in your Christian walk. This six-session study examines six biblical traits found in growing disciples. Without becoming legalistic, it will help you evaluate your relationship with Christ and make needed adjustments to advance towards spiritual maturity.

- Identify areas for growth in your faith.
- Develop healthy habits to spur spiritual growth.
- Learn to engage God's Word more deeply.
- Pursue a lifestyle of continual repentance and humility.
- Develop a hunger for lost friends to know Jesus.
- Align your priorities with God's priorities.
- Engage in the mission of the church to share the gospel.
- Understand the importance of sound teaching.